Praise for

"This deceptively simple little gem will be read and reread many times, each reading uncovering a further milestone on the journey of facing and living with cancer. Gone is the violence and battle imagery, replaced by the hope and peace found in a garden; the garden of knowledge contained in our treatments, in the garden of our loves and friendships and in our own hearts. And in a little monkey called Nutmeg."

~**Anne Richards,** living with cancer

"Worley is a gifted writer. She shares her fears and triumphs in this lighthearted, touching, funny and deeply moving story of her personal journey undergoing cancer treatment with the help of her fuzzy friend, Nutmeg. I would highly recommend this book to anyone undergoing cancer treatment or treatment for other serious medical conditions. This book would also be a useful read for family members and friends as well."

~**Dr. Judy Chiasson,**
Doctor of Acupuncture and Oriental Medicine

"I found Hope Lives in a Garden a touching and whimsical book. Helen Worley has written a caring, careful and thought-provoking story and her choice of gardening as a metaphor is better than that of war to approach a cancer diagnosis."

~**Larry Collins, M.D.,**
President, Vancouver Medical Association;
Past Member, Palliative Care Steering Committee.

Hope Lives in a Garden

A tale of whimsy and healing

by
Helen Worley

Color illustrations by

Georgia Donovan

Hope Lives in a Garden
—A tale of whimsy and healing

Color Illustrations by Georgia Donovan

Print ISBN: 978-0-9854867-0-9
E-book ISBN: 978-0-98548670-9

Helen Worley: helenworley.com
Georgia Donovan: georgiadonovanpetraits.com

Book design, prepress & ebook design:
Kate Weisel, weiselcreative.com
Typeset in Brioso Pro.

A Few Words...

My dream in writing this tale was to share what I have learned about the power of whimsy and gratefulness in healing. I also wanted to challenge the predominant metaphor of fighting as a way to approach a cancer diagnosis, offering gardening as a holistic alternative.

My goal is to raise money to support three groups who are working to help people who are living with cancer and to discover ways to prevent it. All proceeds from the sale of *Hope Lives in a Garden* will go to:

- The Callanish Society, Vancouver, BC, Canada (www.callanishsociety.org)
- Lung Cancer Research and Education Fund, University of Washington, Seattle, WA
- PeaceHealth St. Joseph Center for Integrative Cancer Care, Bellingham, WA

Many people played pivotal roles in this book's creation.

Joan Bubbs: your gift of Nutmeg opened the door to a new understanding of healing.

Arron Henson: you called Nutmeg a part of the healing team, and with the other members of the team at the PeaceHealth Radiation Center taught me how whimsy helps you do your vital work.

Drs Marta Kazymyra, Cary Kaufman, Bill Rubin, Stuart Thorson, David Baker, Michael Taylor and Douglas Wood: without your skills, wisdom and caring my story would be much different. Thank you.

Laura Kalpakian: your support and encouragement was instrumental in getting Nutmeg's story into the world.

Janie Brown: you and the people at the Callanish Society showed me the power of a safe place where deep healing can occur and that it is okay—more than okay, good and necessary—to be oneself with all that entails.

The Callanish Eight: precious and unique friends, you inspire me to keep on blooming, even as we mourn the loss of one flower, Agnes Kwasnicka.

Georgia Donovan: dear friend and gifted artist, Nutmeg comes alive on these pages because of you. Thank for your gift of the color illustrations which grace this book.

LeRoy Worley: husband, lover, friend, companion and the one who makes me smile, you are my rock.

Nutmeg: I gaze into your eyes and know you are an animated inanimate creature. You know how to **be** in the fullest sense of that word and you let me **be** too. You are a treasure.

Choose me! *Please* choose me! I wish I could catch her eye somehow, but my shelf is at the top of the display cabinet in the store. She probably won't even see me. Oh choose me!

I wish I could wave. But I can't. I'm only a little stuffed monkey, all furry, chocolate-brown and caramel-tan. I have black eyes, standy-up ears, a droopy-down head and a not very long tail.

Hey, she sees me! She's picking me up and

taking me to the cash register! Off comes the price tag! I'm being bundled up in pink tissue and put in a gift bag.

I'm so excited! Who will I belong to? Where am I going? What is going to happen to me?

The car stops and, still in my bag, I am carried inside. "I have a gift for you, something to make you smile, Helen," says the woman who brought me here. Her voice is warm.

As I come out of the gift bag, I see a lady with fair, freckled skin, and curly reddish hair. Hey, I can already tell I make her happy. Her green eyes sparkle, glisten with tears of joy.

"Oh Joanie, he is adorable! Thank you," Helen says to her friend. Helen sniffs my tummy. "You smell so nice."

I want to giggle, but I can't, of course. She has discovered the nutmeg-scented beanbag in my tummy.

"You also look rather nutmeg-ish. That's your name: Nutmeg," she says. "My name is Helen, Nutmeg, and this is my husband, LeRoy. Say hello."

LeRoy is tall with dark hair and glasses. He says hello, though he looks a little dubious.

Still holding me close Helen walks Joanie to the door to say goodbye. Joanie tells me to take good care of Helen, and I promise I will.

"Let's show Nutmeg the garden, LeRoy," says Helen.

We walk into a large, beautiful space, a lawn surrounded by tall trees and dazzling flowers in wonderful colors and look! A pond. A pond with a waterfall, Helen! That's what I want to shout, but I can't.

"Oh no, look at these weeds," says Helen, putting me in a wicker chair, and bending down to pull and tug on a few weeds. "Wherever you have flowers, there will be weeds. Always."

"Yes," says LeRoy, moving me aside so he can sit down. I end up on his knee. I smile at him.

Helen comes up to both of us. She gives us each a flower she has picked. She keeps the weeds in her other hand. "This cancer is like a weed, LeRoy. It threatens the flowers in the garden. The body is like a garden. I will be doing everything I can, staying vigilant and making sure the flowers can grow."

"I will help you, Helen," says LeRoy. He's rewarded with a kiss.

And I will help you, too, Helen! And I get a quick kiss too! Helen tells me I am special. She is special too.

They take me inside and Helen places me on a bed beside Fuzzy, a very fuzzy bear and Cupcake, a small white bear with cinnamon ears and nose. We make friends quickly in our secret, silent way.

The next day Helen picks me off the bed and takes me to the car. "We are buddies,

Nutmeg, and we are off on an adventure."

You bet, Helen! I like adventures. She even puts the seat belt around me in the passenger seat so I will be safe.

As we drive, she tells me we are going to the hospital. She will have radiation treatments for breast cancer. She had surgery, and now she needs radiation. I listen, nodding seriously with my droopy-down head.

The hospital is a huge building with many windows and a long covered walk. We go to the Cancer Center Radiation Unit, and at the front desk we are greeted by a woman named Liz.

"Who is your friend, Helen? Usually only kids bring stuffed animals to treatment."

"Oh, Nutmeg is much more than a stuffed animal. He's my buddy," says Helen. "Here, give him a handshake, Liz."

"He smells of nutmeg!"

"Yes," says Helen, smiling at me. "He is an original. He'll come with me every time."

"All thirty-five radiation treatments?" asks Liz.

Thirty-five! I gulp. I can feel Helen tense up too. I snuggle closer.

"Yes, all thirty-five. This is the first," Helen explains to me.

"OK," says Liz, "we'll be seeing you both every day for the next seven weeks. These radiation treatments are to help prevent any recurrence of your breast cancer, Helen. You had the operation, of course, but these are a sort of insurance."

"Like preventive work in a garden," says Helen.

"Yes," says Liz brightly. "That's a fine way to say it."

We follow Liz into a very large room with a big machine in the centre looming over a raised platform bed. Helen lies down on the frame molded especially for her while Liz helps and adjusts.

"I want to keep Nutmeg with me," says Helen.

And I want to stay.

"Of course." Liz tucks me between Helen's left hand and her side. "Are you ready?"

Helen says she is, so I have to be brave too.

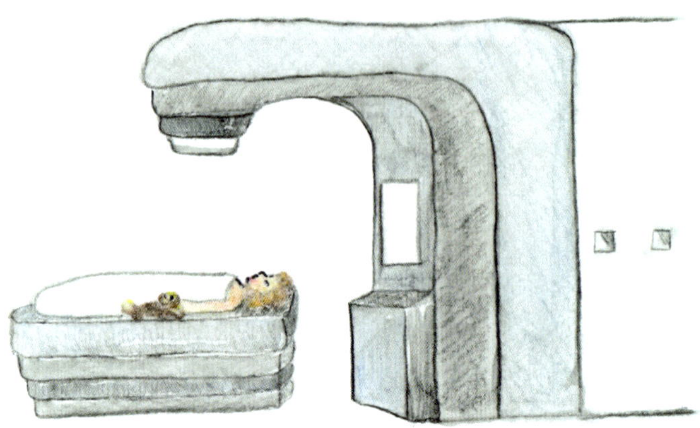

Above us the machine moves into position. Liz leaves us alone with the machine that makes clicking sounds, powerful rays zapping Helen's breast where once she had cancer. We are alone and Helen whispers, "Thank you for this healing power. Thank you for the people who work to make this possible. I pray for strength to heal."

Only I can hear her.

This pattern is repeated every day: I know I am helping Helen, and maybe my happy expression and huggable nature are important to the staff too. There's a whole team of technicians, but mostly we see Liz and Arron. They always hug me before they place me next to Helen on the platform. The machine lumbers into position. Then it's just Helen and me. I always snuggle close and Helen always whispers her prayer of thanks and hope.

On the last of the thirty-five days, after her last treatment, I perch on the counter while Helen signs some papers. Everyone congratulates her.

Suddenly Arron picks me up, holds me high overhead and we scurry around the corner!

"Nutmeg's been monkey-napped," Helen splutters.

"You have to leave Nutmeg here, Helen! He is part of the healing team," Arron says from our hiding place.

That's true, but I must stay with Helen. I'm happy when he places me back in her arms.

Everyone waves as we walk through the doors for the last time. I wave too. Goodbye Arron. Goodbye Liz. Goodbye Cancer Center Radiation Unit. We're all through here!

When we get in the car, Helen doesn't start right up. She puts her head back against the seat. She draws a deep breath. She picks me up and holds me. I can feel her tears. That's fine, Helen. I can absorb your tears. I wrap my little arms close around her.

"Oh Nutmeg," she says, wiping her eyes. "We did it." She put me back in my seat and fastens my seat belt. She shakes my hand.

We did it, Helen! Now we can go home.

For a long time I stay on the bed with my friends, Fuzzy and Cupcake. Almost two months. Then one day Helen picks me up and says we're going for another hospital adventure. I am ready. I don't know what kind of adventure, but I am always ready to absorb laughter, tears or fears, to be present and part of healing.

We go to a different place in the hospital—Pre-Op. Helen is here for an operation. She will have a cervical fusion of the spine. She and LeRoy and I wait for the doctor to talk to us. I sit in Helen's lap. She has one hand on me, and with her other hand, she pats LeRoy's arm.

The doctor says to us, "We will do an incision on the right side of your neck, gently pull apart the muscles and blood vessels and then fuse three vertebrae."

Don't worry, Helen, I whisper. I will stay with you. Just like I did in the radiation room. I am not afraid. I will help you.

Helen must have heard me. She turns to me, says gently, "You can't come with me this time, Nutmeg. Will you take care of LeRoy? He needs you too."

"We'll be fine." says LeRoy, kissing her forehead.

He and I go to the lounge. I sit on the chair beside LeRoy who is reading a book. Don't worry, LeRoy, I try to tell him. You are not alone. I am here to help you and Helen. Every so often he tickles my head.

A long time later, hours, LeRoy carries me up to the bright and sunny room. Helen lies in the bed. Her neck is wrapped in bandages, and she looks tired, but she is happy to see us, both of us. LeRoy puts me beside her and she pats my nutmeg tummy.

A nurse adjusting a monitor beside Helen frowns at me. He says, "What is this? A stuffed monkey?"

"Not just any stuffed monkey," says Helen.

"This is Nutmeg. He's experienced in hospitals. He stayed with me through thirty-five days of radiation."

And I will stay with her here too, I tell that frowning nurse. I will always be present!

All night long I lay beside Helen. She sleeps, but I stay awake giving her lots of love and comfort. The next day the doctor tells her she can go home earlier than planned. She is doing so well.

"I'm sure it's because Nutmeg is helping me heal," says Helen.

"He is a whimsical little monkey," the doctor says.

"Yes," says Helen, "he has the healing power of whimsy."

I am part of her recovery at home too. I go out in the garden with her. I sit with her in the sunshine. I tell her: don't try to weed this garden, Helen! You need to slow down. Take care of yourself while you get well.

She smiles and sits beside me, reaches out and ruffles my fur. "Well I'm going to spray these roses, Nutmeg. It's just a soapy solution, but it keeps the roses from being infested with nasty aphids and bugs. And then, I promise you, I'll rest."

While I watch her, a sparrow comes up and perches on the chair. He looks like he might want my fuzzy fur for his nest. Shoo! I tell him. He looks surprised that a stuffed monkey can communicate, but he flies away.

A year has come and gone when suddenly Helen swoops into the room and plucks me off the bed. Another adventure?

"We need to be weeding the garden again, Nutmeg," she says as she packs her book-and-sweater bag. "We have to protect the flowers from the weeds."

Of course, I think. But we are not going outside to the garden. Instead, she pins a pink ribbon to my chest.

"This is a breast cancer ribbon, Nutmeg. You get one because you helped me through that. I survived the operation and the radiation, but when I had breast cancer, they found a mysterious spot on my lung." She picks me up and holds me close. "It is malignant, Nutmeg, and I have to have another operation. This one is for lung cancer."

I feel her breath against my furry cheek. We both know this IS serious.

In my own way, I say to her, I will go through this adventure too, Helen. We will be together. You can count on me.

Helen nods. "I can't imagine going through it without you."

I sit in Helen's lap again while LeRoy drives us. I am a little afraid. But I am brave too. It's a long ride. To a distant hospital. Even bigger and with more windows.

We three go inside to a reception desk. I sit there watching when suddenly Helen says to the clerk. "This is Nutmeg, and he'll be with me."

"Oh, then he most certainly must have his own ID tag," says the clerk.

Helen smiles. "He will never get lost."

I will never get lost. But I do fall over. The clerk smiles and puts an ID tag around my neck, careful so that my pink ribbon for breast cancer will show.

I thank her, even if she can't hear me, and she tells Helen I am all set now.

But we have a long wait, the three of us in a pre-op cubicle. Helen keeps me in her lap. She holds LeRoy's hand and they chat softly. Finally a doctor comes in. He wears a white coat and a serious expression, but he is calm. Me, I am serious and calm too.

"The operation will take quite a while," says the doctor. "We'll actually do three procedures. I am not anticipating any problems, but we have to be certain. It will take about six and a half hours."

Six and half hours! Oh Helen! I look up at her with all the love and whimsy and hugs and healing I can possibly muster. I want to come with her. She pats my nutmeg-tummy and asks if I will look after LeRoy again. She knows how much I want to be with her. She knows too I will take good care of LeRoy

When the nurse comes in, LeRoy hugs Helen one last time and puts me in the book-bag, and we leave. I'm here, Helen! I call out as best I can. I'm here and I am with you. Even though I'm really with LeRoy.

This time I do not sit on the chair beside him. There are too many people in the room for me to have my own chair. They watch television. I stay in the book bag beside LeRoy as he reads. Or tries to. He cannot read the book for very long. He puts it back in the bag, being very careful of me. We are both thinking of Helen.

A long while passes and then LeRoy carries me in the bag down another long hall. When at last he brings me out, I am bewildered. Is that Helen lying there? There are so many tubes going into her, and there are towers beside her, and oxygen tubes around her head.

LeRoy gently hands me to her. “Here is your friend,” he says.

“Oh, Nutmeg,” Helen whispers. Her green eyes are not bright, but she smiles.

Dear Helen I tell her.

LeRoy holds her hand. “The doctor says it went well. The tumor was quite large. They took the whole lobe of your lung. But the doctor is very pleased with how everything went. Now you have to rest and get well.”

Helen nods sleepily. I snuggle close to her.

I will help her heal. I will be with her through this.

And that is true. Helen and I are moved out of the recovery room to our own room. I stay with her after LeRoy leaves for the night. The nurse shows her how to use a little pump he puts in her hand. “It’s pain medication,” he says. “Use it whenever you need it. That’s what it’s for. Who is your friend?”

“Nutmeg,” says Helen before she drifts off to sleep.

Yes Helen?

“Shhh,” says the nurse, leaving me tucked in her arms. “You rest, Helen.”

It is a difficult and restless night. She wakes up often and uses the pump for the pain medication. She whispers to me that she is grateful.

Grateful, Helen? This might be an adventure, but it's a pretty scary one. (I don't tell her that, but I think it.)

"I am grateful for LeRoy's love, for family, for all my friends and so much more."

Oh. Yes, Helen. Me too.

She wakes again in the night. "I'm grateful, Nutmeg. Grateful for breast cancer."

Really Helen?

"Can you imagine? If I hadn't had breast cancer, this lung cancer would never have been found till it was too late."

I am grateful too, Helen. See my pink ribbon?

"I'm grateful for the doctors and nurses, radiologists, and other specialists… who have all worked so hard so that I can be well again. And you. I am grateful for you too."

Thank you Helen. I think I might cry. Good thing I'm just a little stuffed monkey and I cannot cry.

But when others cry, I can absorb their tears. I snuggle in closer to her, my furry cheek next to her cheek.

She wakes again a few hours later, and I think she needs the pain medication again, but instead, she lies there for a bit.

"Nutmeg, we are going for a walk."

Really Helen? It's four a.m.

"I am getting out of bed and taking a walk."

Helen, you just had surgery yesterday, you shouldn't—

"Today down the hall. Tomorrow out in the garden."

Now, that's an adventure! But I can't go along because there's no place for me on the walker. The nurse goes with her. Helen puts me up against the pillow, and I wave bye bye.

"Well maybe not tomorrow into the garden," she concedes when she returns. She is tired. "That may take a little while."

But you did it, Helen, I tell her. You walked.

"Yes, Nutmeg. I did it. I will do it again tomorrow."

Let's get some sleep. Helen agrees.

The next day and the days after that, LeRoy comes to visit. He always bring her a latte, her favorite drink. He always says hello to me and asks me of I'm taking good care of Helen. Of course I am! We watch TV, baseball and golf.

Friends come to visit. They bring little snacks and flowers and cheer.

As the hospital shifts change, the nurses introduce me to each other. They all pick me up and smell my nutmeg tummy. Helen says she relies on me. They can see why.

One morning we have a new nurse, Pam who chats while she monitors the medication flowing through the tubes. "Helen, I've been reading your chart, and what a year you've had! Breast cancer and radiation. Cervical fusion of your spine. And now major surgery for lung cancer. After all that, you were up and walking around at four in the morning the day after surgery. No one expected that! You are a real fighter, Helen."

"That's kind of you," says Helen, "but, you know, I don't see cancer as something to be battled. To be fought. I don't like warlike imagery. I didn't use it when I had breast cancer and I won't use it with lung cancer either."

"Well what else can you call it but a fight?"

Helen thinks for a few minutes. I think with her.

"I think of it like a garden. My body is a garden, with all the varieties of plants that come together to make a beautiful garden. You can't have a garden without weeds. You have to tend a garden, coax the plants to life and protect the seeds so they can sprout and push and come up through the soil, and reach for the sunlight. Storms come, weeds crop up, nasty bugs latch on to new shoots. So to have a garden you have to spend hours, not just planting, but weeding and pruning, spraying and fertilizing."

You are so right, Helen, I tell her. She pats my tummy. She knows I know.

"Cancer is like a weed and this surgery is a weeding operation," she goes on, "getting rid of the choking weed so that the garden can flourish. And then we'll fertilize with fresh air and exercise and good food and the garden will be restored. Gardens are places of beauty and strength, constantly changing and being renewed. That's how I like to think of myself — never static, always growing, resilient and full of life—and ready to blossom."

Pam looks sort of stunned. "You learn all that from your little monkey friend?"

"He has certainly helped."

I lean in against Helen, and she pats my furry head. She is alive, always growing, never static. I am here to help.

That night Helen tosses and wakes, and I wonder if she's going to take another walk. Or maybe she needs more pain meds. But she doesn't press the button.

"Nutmeg," she says softly.

Yes, Helen?

"I can't help feeling that I've missed something. What am I supposed to learn from this experience? What's the message? What's my body trying to tell me? Where's the gift in this?"

I was a gift, Helen. But I know that's not what she means. She means that from all of our adventures, she is supposed to learn something. But what? I do not have answers. I listen. The hospital room is lit only by glowing monitors and the light under the door.

Helen turns to me on the pillow. "I have been given another chance at life, Nutmeg. I do not want to waste it."

I know there are times when Helen is overwhelmed, and wants to cry. I know tears can help and I can absorb her tears. I offer hope. I accept secrets, even secret fears. I give love. Though I am simply a little stuffed monkey full of whimsy, I know that she relies on me. I gaze at her. I tell her: You will not waste it. Go to sleep, Helen I will keep my eyes open all night long and watch over everything.

Five days later the doctor comes into her

room. He seems happy. "You have done so well, Helen that you can go home. We are all impressed."

"Don't forget Nutmeg," says Helen. "He helped."

"I could never forget him. He is part of the healing team," says the doctor. And he shakes my paw.

LeRoy drives us home. Though it is a long journey, we are all three happy to be together. She has me in her arms.

Healing doesn't happen overnight. Weeks pass. Helen keeps me nearby. I am sending healing energies, and she knows it. Sometimes she picks me up and hugs me for no reason. I know she needs my warmth, my understanding. Even though I'm inanimate, I can be animated and hug her back. As the days pass her eyes begin to sparkle again.

Sometimes we go out into the garden together. She takes walks, and I sit on the wicker chair, cheering her on.

She bends down carefully and pulls up a couple of chickweeds. She picks a daisy and brings it back to me. She puts it against my fur and sits down beside me. "Nutmeg, you are such a gift. You are present."

You mean like here, present, Helen? Or that I was a present from Joanie?

"Both," she says. "You are present in the present. You were a gift and you are a gift.

People relax around you and smile even when they're not happy. Haven't you noticed? Especially adults. They're sometimes more afraid than children. Afraid to show emotions, but they don't need to be afraid around you. Is it the smell of nutmeg, I wonder?" She winks.

She knows the smell of nutmeg isn't the whole answer. In my secret, silent way, I can absorb fear, and joy and sadness, anxiety and uncertainty.

"There's something else about joy and sadness, Nutmeg. They meet in the same heartbeat and together they spell hope." She smiles.

Hope is like a flower in the garden. Hope blooms even among the weeds. Helen tilts her head back, closes her eyes and lets the sunshine play over her face. Me too.

About the Author

Indefatigable optimist Helen Worley lives near a pond in the small city of Blaine, Washington, just south of the US/Canada border, and an hour away from her hometown of Vancouver, BC, Canada.

In her work Helen spent many hours with cancer patients; she cared for her first husband during his three bouts of the disease, nursing him at home during his last days; she then faced two separate cancer diagnoses herself. Her insights come from deep personal experience.

Helen shares her enthusiasm for life in her writing and photographs, being constantly on the alert for the extraordinary in the ordinary.

Hope Lives in a Garden is her first book.

To see her art and to read her blog, visit helenworley.com.

About the Illustrator

Georgia Donovan finds her bliss in doing what she enjoys most… creating art. Her work is characterized by her quirky sense of humor and whimsical approach. She is especially noted for her commissioned pet portraits. She lives in Blaine, WA.

For more creatures to fall in love with visit her website: georgiadonovanpetraits.com.

Made in the USA
Charleston, SC
20 October 2012